CAREERS ON THE FRONT LINE

SPECIAL FORCES CAREERS

SARAH EASON

CRABTREE
PUBLISHING COMPANY
WWW.CRABTREEBOOKS.COM

T0021045

CRABTREE
PUBLISHING COMPANY
WWW.CRABTREEBOOKS.COM

Author: Sarah Eason
Editors: Jennifer Sanderson
Ellen Rodger
Proofreader: Tracey Kelly
Indexer: Tracey Kelly
Editorial director:
Kathy Middleton
Interior design: Emma DeBanks
Cover and logo design:
Katherine Berti
Photo research: Rachel Blount
Print coordinator:
Katherine Berti
Consultant: David Hawksett

Written, developed, and produced for Crabtree
Publishing by Calcium Creative Ltd.

Photo Credits:
t=Top, tr=Top Right, tl=Top Left
Inside: Shutterstock: Getmilitaryphotos: pp. 20, 21,
23, 29; PRESSLAB: pp. 3, 19, 28t, 28b; U.S. Air Force:
Master Sgt. Brian Lamar: p. 17; U.S. Air National
Guard: Staff Sgt. Joshua Horton: p. 5; Wikimedia
Commons: Paul Abell/AP Images for U.S. Army
Reserve: p. 12; Maj. David Butler, U.S. Army: p. 7; DoD
photo by Tech. Sgt. Cecilio M. Ricardo Jr., U.S. Air
Force: p. 6; ISAF Headquarters Public Affairs Office/
Master Corporal Angela Abbey, Canadian Forces
Combat Camera: p. 15; Capt. Nicholas Mannweiler:
p. 24; Tom Michele: p. 27; Starry, Donn A. Mounted
combat in Vietnam. Department of the Army: p. 11;
Maria L. Taylor: p. 8; U.S. Air Force/Airman 1st Class
Christopher Callaway: p. 16; U.S. Air Force photo by
Senior Airman Julianne Showalter: pp. 1, 4; U.S. Army:
p 13; U.S. Army photo by 2nd. Lt. Christopher Molaro:
p. 25; Steven Young: p. 9. Front cover: Shutterstock

Library and Archives Canada Cataloguing in Publication

Title: Special forces careers / Sarah Eason.
Names: Eason, Sarah, author.
Description: Series statement: Careers on the front line |
Includes bibliographical references and index.
Identifiers: Canadiana (print) 20200283944 |
Canadiana (ebook) 20200283952 |
ISBN 9780778781424 (hardcover) |
ISBN 9780778781486 (softcover) |
ISBN 9781427125828 (HTML)
Subjects: LCSH: Special forces (Military science)—Vocational
guidance—United States—Juvenile literature. | LCSH:
Special forces (Military science)—United States—Recruiting,
enlistment, etc.—Juvenile literature. | LCSH: Special forces
(Military science)—Vocational guidance—Canada—Juvenile
literature. | LCSH: Special forces (Military science)—Canada—
Recruiting, enlistment, etc.—Juvenile literature.
Classification: LCC U262 .H83 2020 | DDC j356/.16023—dc23

Library of Congress Cataloging-in-Publication Data

Names: Eason, Sarah, author.
Title: Special forces careers / Sarah Eason.
Description: New York : Crabtree Publishing Company, [2021]
| Series: Careers on the front line | Includes index.
Identifiers: LCCN 2020029707 (print) |
LCCN 2020029708 (ebook) |
ISBN 9780778781424 (hardcover) |
ISBN 9780778781486 (paperback) |
ISBN 9781427125828 (ebook)
Subjects: LCSH: Special forces (Military science)--Vocational
guidance--Juvenile literature. | Special operations (Military
science)--Vocational guidance--Juvenile literature.
Classification: LCC U262 .E27 2021 (print) | LCC U262 (ebook)
| DDC 356/.16023--dc23
LC record available at https://lccn.loc.gov/2020029707
LC ebook record available at https://lccn.loc.gov/2020029708

Crabtree Publishing Company

www.crabtreebooks.com   1-800-387-7650

Printed in the U.S.A./082020/CG20200710

Copyright © **2021 CRABTREE PUBLISHING COMPANY.** All rights reserved. No part of this publication may be reproduced, stored in a retrieval
system, or be transmitted in any form or by any means, electronic, mechanical, photocopying, recording, or otherwise, without the prior written
permission of Crabtree Publishing Company. In Canada: We acknowledge the financial support of the Government of Canada through the Canada
Book Fund for our publishing activities.

Published in Canada
Crabtree Publishing
616 Welland Ave.
St. Catharines, Ontario
L2M 5V6

Published in the United States
Crabtree Publishing
347 Fifth Ave
Suite 1402-145
New York, NY 10016

Published in the United Kingdom
Crabtree Publishing
Maritime House
Basin Road North, Hove
BN41 1WR

Published in Australia
Crabtree Publishing
3 Charles Street
Coburg North
VIC, 3058

CONTENTS

DANGEROUS AND DEADLY

The Special Operations Forces (SOF) are part of a country's armed forces or military. The armed forces include the army, navy, and air force. SOF soldiers are trained to go on missions that are often secretive and require special skills. These highly trained soldiers may have to leave their family and friends at a moment's notice to take on a life-threatening mission.

THE U.S. SPECIAL OPERATIONS FORCES

The U.S. SOF are made up of different groups that can work together or separately. Each group has a particular skill, but they all specialize in **classified** missions, such as **counterterrorism** and **hostage** rescue. The Army Special Forces, also called the Green Berets, are called to action in any situation that threatens the safety of U.S. property or citizens. Other SOF include the Army Rangers, who are called on for air attacks, such as seizing enemy airfields; Delta Force, a top secret unit; and the Navy SEALs. The SEALs fight on land and in the air, but are also specially trained to deal with any sea or water missions, such as **minesweeping** in harbors and rivers.

SOF soldiers have to be ready to parachute into jungles, deserts, and the ocean on rescue missions.

This search-and-rescue dog is being prepared for a parachute jump.

CANADIAN SPECIAL OPERATIONS FORCES

The Canadian Special Operations Forces Command (CANSOFCOM) has four fighting units: Joint Task Force 2 (JTF 2); Canadian Special Operations Regiment (CSOR); 427 Special Operations Aviation Squadron (SOAS); and Canadian Joint Incident Response Unit—**Chemical**, **Biological**, **Radiological**, and **Nuclear** (CJIRU-CBRN). As with the U.S. SOF, these Canadian soldiers are highly trained to deal with dangerous and top secret situations. The fifth CANSOFCOM unit is the Canadian Special Operations Training Centre (CSOTC), which trains CANSOFCOM soldiers.

Your FRONTLINE Career

Look for "Your Frontline Career" boxes. They highlight the skills and strengths needed for specific SOF careers. They can be used to help you decide whether a career in the SOF is for you and what roles might suit you best.

FRONTLINE MISSIONS

The **personnel** of the SOF are some of the toughest, most highly trained soldiers in the world. They go on dangerous, secret, and deadly missions that no other military units are trained to do. The SOF are used to gather intelligence, or secret information, about enemy countries that could be a threat. They rescue hostages, work to track down **terrorists** or drug **warlords** in **hostile** environments, and perform a wide range of **undercover** operations.

ENEMY TERRITORY

SOF usually carry out missions behind enemy lines and in secret. They often work in units of four or five soldiers. In **reconnaissance** missions, soldiers have to go deep into enemy territory with no protection or support from tanks or helicopters. Their aim is to collect information that will help other military units make surprise attacks. For example, they may report on how well equipped the enemy is and exactly where enemy fighters are. This information will help other units plan and carry out more accurate and successful operations.

SOF officers may be sent on a mission into a dense jungle, so they train specifically for that.

SURPRISE ATTACK

SOF also carry out Direct Action missions. These are attacks that happen over a short period of time. They are planned to take the enemy by surprise. They are used to capture or destroy very specific enemy equipment, such as weapons, or to rescue captured prisoners. SOF units can operate small-scale raids, trap and **ambush** the enemy, or **sabotage** enemy operations. They are also used on top secret missions, including ones that require them to enter a foreign country without permission.

Students at the Special Forces Underwater Operations School in Florida train for their dive qualifications in a pool before they move on to open waters.

COUNTERTERRORISM

Terrorism is a big threat in today's world. Counterterrorism missions respond to terrorist activities overseas. SOF units hunt down terrorist leaders and units that threaten the safety of civilians, or ordinary people, at home and overseas. Missions can include ways to stop attacks, such as destroying terrorist weapons and tracking down terrorist leaders, and rescuing hostages captured by terrorists. These missions can also include training counterterrorism teams in other countries.

TOP TRAINING

*SOF soldiers must undergo the most difficult training the military has to offer. Fitness, health, and strength levels have to be at their highest. Specialized training includes advanced warfare **tactics**, decision-making, problem-solving, and mission planning. Some SOF training includes learning about other **cultures** and speaking a foreign language.*

THE GREEN BERETS

The U.S. Army SOF units are known as the Green Berets because of the color of the berets, or hats, they wear. These soldiers are trained to fight on land, at sea, and in the air. They can cross enemy lines unseen, hunt down the world's most dangerous terrorists, and train **guerilla** armies in hostile and threatening surroundings. They may have to parachute into enemy territory or swim through freezing, rough oceans in the middle of the night to reach their target. They are brave and fearless.

SUPER FIT

To start training to become a Green Beret, a person must be super fit. Candidates should be able to complete a 2-mile (3.2 km) run in 12 to 14 minutes, do 100 sit-ups in 2 minutes, and do 100 push-ups in 2 minutes. Green Berets also need high-level day and night **navigation** skills. They learn survival skills for different environments, such as rain forests, mountain regions, and deserts. Survival skills include how to set animal traps for food, finding water, recognizing poisonous plants, building shelters, and making fires.

The Green Berets risk their lives each time they go on a mission. These Green Berets salute a soldier who died in battle.

Green Berets train hard! Here, they are in rifle training, preparing for raids on dangerous drug traffickers.

SUPERSMART

Green Berets also have to be supersmart. The success of a mission will often depend on the Green Berets working with local people. To gain the trust of local people and leaders, soldiers must learn about the politics, language, culture, religion, and customs of the country where they are working. Green Beret soldiers do not just win by fighting. Often, long **negotiations** are needed. Green Beret warriors are trained to quickly analyze a situation and deal with it in the best way possible, which may be by talking, walking away, or fighting.

THE A-TEAM

*The Green Berets usually work in a small team of 12 soldiers called the Alpha Team (A-Team). The team is made up of commanders and operations and intelligence sergeants, as well as weapons, communications, medical, and engineering sergeants. Depending on their mission, they may also have specialized training in parachuting, ocean diving, polar environments, and land vehicle warfare, such as tanks and **armored vehicles**.*

Chalmers Archer:
SAVING LIVES

In 1952, African American soldier Chalmers Archer was one of the first men to train at the then-named Psychological Warfare Center and School, a part of the newly formed U.S. Army's Special Forces. Psychological warfare has since become an important part of SOF military tactics. Psychological warfare uses tactics such as sending out messages on social media deliberately worded to make people behave in a certain way. For example, this might be sending out information to make the enemy feel scared or threatened, so that they do something they would not normally do.

Your FRONTLINE Career

Is Working at the Psychological Warfare Center for You?

Sounds Great
- Learning skills to survive in any environment, from forests to deserts and mountains
- Learning new languages and understanding different cultures and customs
- Being pushed mentally and physically

Things to Think About
- Missions are dangerous and often take place in extreme circumstances
- Negotiating with local people and fighting forces takes patience and understanding of the enemy
- Having to make quick and difficult decisions, such as whether it is better to stay and fight or walk away.

Archer's first assignments with the Psychological Warfare Center were top secret missions to Thailand and Taiwan. He was then sent to the Vietnam front line with the 1st Special Forces Group in 1957. The war in Vietnam was fought between North Vietnam and South Vietnam. **Communist** countries including the Soviet Union and China supported North Vietnam. South Vietnam was supported by the United States, Australia, and other anti-communist countries. The war lasted from 1955 to 1975. The mission was twofold. Archer and his men had to win over the local people by using **propaganda** to turn them against the communist countries. Once local people were on their side, the mission was to build an army of **resistance fighters** that would turn against the communist government.

Archer's team of Green Berets worked with the Central Intelligence Agency (CIA). The CIA is a government organization that collects and analyzes information from around the world to help keep the United States safe from enemy threats. Archer trained the original SOF teams in the South Vietnamese Army and took part in many classified missions. His unit suffered some of the first casualties of the war when its captain was killed and other soldiers in the unit were badly injured.

When Archer retired from the Army in 1967, he went back to school to build on the experience he had gained as a member of the 1st Special Forces Group. He completed his master's degree in education and took degrees in counseling and psychology.

Chalmers Archer would have worked with soldiers such as these during the Vietnam War.

EXTREME OPERATORS

In Canada, Joint Task Force 2 (JTF 2), stands ready and waiting to leap into action whenever the Canadian Army or government needs their skills and expertise. The soldiers serving in this SOF unit are highly trained professionals who perform a range of top secret missions, including hostage rescue and protecting Canadians at home and overseas against terrorist threats. Similarly, in the United States, the **elite** Army Ranger regiment soldiers are trained in large-scale special operations in the air, at sea, and on land.

TOP OF THE RANGE

Army Rangers have to pass some of the toughest training in the world. This prepares soldiers for extreme and challenging situations, and includes being disciplined to eat only one meal a day quickly and in silence. This is to train soldiers for times when they will have to survive on little food and eat it in difficult situations. They are also allowed only a few hours of sleep. The training is divided into three phases. First, the Crawl or Benning Phase increases physical fitness, mental toughness, and tactical skills. Second, the Walk or Mountain Phase teaches soldiers how to fight in mountainous regions and develop command skills. The third Run or Swamp Phase in the swamps of Florida pushes soldiers to their limits. It tests how they behave and cope with extreme mental and physical stress.

In 2015, the first female soldiers graduated Ranger School. They are Kristen Griest, Lisa Jaster, and Shaye Haver.

SECRET FORCES

The Rangers are all volunteers, as are soldiers who fight for JTF 2. Volunteers for JTF 2 are taken from the Canadian Army, Air Force, and Navy. There are six units based across Canada. Each unit consists of fighters called assaulters and **support personnel**, such as medics. JTF 2 was set up to respond to terrorist situations, **natural disasters**, and **humanitarian crises**. Most of their missions are top secret, but we know that they have fought terrorists in Afghanistan, provided protection for the Canadian Embassy and airport in Haiti during political upheaval, and helped rescue three **peace workers** held hostage in Iraq.

FEARLESS FIGHTERS

Individual soldiers have to be able to trust and depend on the skills and mental strength of their team members. Unit members have to be able to keep calm and make quick decisions in all situations, and work together toward one goal. If a unit member is injured, the rest of the team has to help the injured soldier back to base and do that soldier's work as well as their own. JTF 2 and Rangers have to be loyal, brave, committed, and strong. They need to be good at planning, leading and following, and problem-solving.

All Rangers can be called to a top secret, highly sensitive, and dangerous mission with 18 hours' notice.

Band of Sisters:
SERVING THEIR COUNTRY

During the war against terrorism in Afghanistan, the Rangers sent in their female special operatives. In Afghanistan, it is not acceptable for the local women to speak to men who are not members of their close family, such as a brother or husband. The U.S. SOF commanders believed that the way to win the war in Afghanistan was through knowledge of what was happening on the ground. Local women could be a huge source of such knowledge, but how could the male soldiers find out this vital information?

The answer was to send out a team of female soldiers with the training to fight alongside the Rangers. After a selection process known as the "100 hours of hell," around 20 women were selected from across the Army, Navy, and Air Force. They all had to be "fierce, athletic, and absolutely determined." In 2010, these female warriors were formed into groups called cultural support teams, which would work alongside the SOF fighters in dangerous combat zones. Their role was to build a bond with the women and gain their trust, so they could search the women and their homes in a way that the male Rangers could not. They were also able to mix with local women and children to gather information. This information could be used to help the Rangers and other SOF accomplish their operations.

Your FRONTLINE Career

Is Being on a Cultural Support Team for You?

Sounds Great
- Traveling to different countries and learning about other people's cultures
- Making important decisions that could be a matter of life and death
- Working as part of a team to achieve a task

Things to Think About
- Keeping your work a secret from friends and family
- Being patient and finding ways to work with local people to build their trust
- Missions are in some of the world's most dangerous war zones

This local information meant that commanders could plan nighttime raids and other military operations, keeping the U.S. soldiers safe and giving the missions a greater chance of success. It also helped build trust between the local Afghan population and the U.S. soldiers. The cultural support teams were kept top secret—even their families in the United States did not know what the women were doing. Many family members thought the women were going out as nurses to set up hospitals for women and children.

However, not all the women survived. In 2011, during a nighttime mission, Lieutenant Ashley White, one of the cultural support team members, and two Rangers were killed when they stepped on buried explosives. Ashley White has since become a U.S. hero. Her story and those of her colleagues has been told in the book, *Ashley's War: The Untold Story of a Team of Women Soldiers on the Special Ops Battlefield*, written by Gayle Tzemach Lemmon.

Like Lieutenant Ashley White and her fellow soldiers, this Canadian soldier is talking to Afghan women to help build bridges between the Army and local people.

NIGHT STALKERS

The U.S. Army's Special Operations Aviation Regiment, Airborne (SOAR-A) is nicknamed the "Night Stalkers." This elite unit flies SOF SEALs and Green Berets to missions around the world. Night Stalker teams, pilots, and crew members can go deep into enemy territory at any time, day or night. They get SOF units in and out of the front line swiftly, quietly, and safely. The Night Stalkers are proud to say that they will be at a target within 30 seconds of any operation time.

NIGHT MISSIONS

A covert, or secret, mission could mean flying at night into a dangerous environment, such as a desert, mountain range, or rain forest. Night Stalker pilots are trained to fly in the most challenging situations, including stormy weather and while being fired at by the enemy. Often, the missions are at night, so the crew flies into unknown territory in pitch blackness. Most Night Stalker helicopters have been **adapted** with special equipment, so that the pilots can see at night. This helps the team assess any dangers and problems, then decide how to deal with them. Other special equipment and adaptations are classified information.

A soldier jumps from a Night Stalker Chinook helicopter as part of a recovery operation.

Night Stalker training is so difficult that the Army has a 30-day course to help soldiers prepare for the actual training.

COMPLETE TEAM

The Night Stalkers include soldiers with specialized training. Some may be trained in life-saving medical skills; others, such as pilots, may have expertise in nighttime navigation and reconnaissance. Pilots are trained in in-flight fueling, **urban** warfare, and landing on a ship's deck. All Night Stalkers are trained in weapons handling and hand-to-hand combat. The crew must work as a team to ensure that missions are completed safely.

QUICK AND TOUGH

Night Stalkers have to be focused and able to deal with any situation. They must be able to make quick decisions and solve problems under dangerous and difficult conditions—the right decision could save lives. They have to be able to handle physical and mental stress and deal with high levels of exhaustion. A crew could fly several missions in one night.

Operation Neptune Spear:
END OF A TYRANT

The Night Stalkers have been involved in some of the world's most dangerous missions. One mission that made world headlines was Operation Neptune Spear. In this covert mission, the United States' most wanted criminal, Osama bin Laden, was finally tracked down and killed.

Your FRONTLINE Career

Is Being a Night Stalker for You?

Sounds Great
• Learning leadership skills and how to be part of a team
• No two days are the same—missions can vary and take place anywhere in the world at any time of the day or night
• Dealing with high levels of stress, as other people's lives depend on you doing a good job

Things to Think About
• Missions may be top secret, so you will not be able to discuss your work with friends or family
• Giving and taking orders are a big part of the job
• Being focused, having quick reactions, and operating under extreme pressure are essential

Osama bin Laden and his terrorist group, al-Qaeda, were responsible for a series of terrorist attacks on the United States that killed thousands of people. The worst was the horrific airplane attack on the World Trade Center in Manhattan, New York City, on September 11, 2001. Nearly 3,000 people were killed in this attack alone.

In September 2010, U.S. intelligence reports claimed that Osama bin Laden had been found and that he was hiding in a **compound** in Pakistan. Operation Neptune Spear was launched to find and capture or kill bin Laden. On the night of the attack, Night Stalkers flew two Black Hawk helicopters into Pakistan carrying Navy SEALs. The helicopters flew beneath the **radar** and from different directions to avoid being detected by the terrorists.

However, as they approached the compound, the tail wing of the Black Hawk hit one of the compound walls, and the helicopter was forced to make a crash landing. The crew destroyed the crashed helicopter as they left the compound, so that its classified technology would not be found and used or copied by the terrorists.

Using night-vision goggles, the SEALs silently entered the compound. As they made their way toward where bin Laden was hiding, they took weapon supplies, cleared away **barricades**, and seized computer hard drives and anything that might contain secret information that could help them destroy al-Qaeda.

Bin Laden was found in a room on the third floor and was shot and killed. Operation Neptune Spear had been a success. Another Chinook helicopter was flown in to fly the soldiers and the body of bin Laden back to the United States. The complete operation had taken 40 minutes. It was one of the most successful SOF missions in the history of the United States.

These SEALs are using night-vision equipment for ground surveillance during a helicopter raid. The SEAL team that carried out the bin Laden mission used similar equipment.

THE SEALS

A Navy SEAL, which stands for Sea, Air, and Land, works in small teams, carrying out missions in some of the world's most hostile environments. A SEAL never works alone, and a SEAL is never left alone. SEALs are unbeatable when it comes to working in thrashing seas, boggy marshes, or fast-flowing rivers. Although SEALs specialize in missions on, under, or near water, they also work in deserts, jungles, and other challenging environments.

TO THE LIMITS

SEAL training pushes members to the limits to make sure that the few who make it through the 30 months of physical and mental challenges will be able to survive on real missions. SEAL recruits have to prove they can cope with the demands and risks of this elite team. They must be able to "swim" 328 feet (100 m) with their hands and feet bound. They have to run across a beach, carrying a 15-foot (4.6 m) rubber boat—called a Zodiac—over their heads while wearing heavy equipment. SEALs are often used in hostage rescues, the capture of targets, and special research. A mission to rescue hostages from enemy territory requires skill, bravery, and teamwork.

Navy SEALs are trained to be able to operate and fight in every environment.

SPECIAL MISSIONS

Many SEAL missions take place in the middle of the night to ensure that enemies are caught by surprise. The darkness hides the SEALs from view, but because they need to see where they are going, they use night-vision goggles. These help them find their way and locate enemy targets in the pitch blackness.

SEALs have to move quickly and quietly on dangerous missions.

LIFESAVERS

Navy SEALs need leadership skills and have to know the importance of working as a team. SEALs do a lot of their work in foreign countries. Having an interest in and understanding of other cultures, such as those in China, India, and Russia, is important. Getting along with the local people in whichever country they find themselves gives the SEALs local knowledge that can save lives.

Marcus Luttrell:

SEAL SURVIVOR

On June 28, 2005, Navy SEAL Marcus Luttrell and his team SEAL Team 10 were assigned to Operation Red Wings, a mission to kill or capture Ahmad Shah (also known as Mohammad Ismail). Shah was a high-ranking **Taliban** leader responsible for killings in eastern Afghanistan and the Hindu Kush mountains.

Your FRONTLINE Career

Is Being a Navy SEAL for You?

Sounds Great
- Being incredibly physically fit
- Mental strength is just as important as physical strength
- Having a specific role and responsibility within a team

Things to Think About
- Training is incredibly tough
- Being able to swim and endure some very difficult and often painful physical challenges
- SEALs need to have a sharp, quick mind and fast reactions

The SEAL team was made up of Luttrell, Michael P. Murphy, Danny Dietz, and Matthew Axelson. Luttrell and Axelson were the team's **snipers**, Dietz was in charge of communications, and Murphy was the team leader. When a group of goat herders stumbled upon the SEALs, the four SEALs immediately took control of the situation and discussed what to do about the herders. After taking a vote and basing their decision on the **Rules of Engagement (ROE)**, Murphy made the final decision to let them go. The herders were subsequently released and disappeared over the mountain ridge. Luttrell believed that they immediately betrayed the team's location to local Taliban forces, and he was right. Within an hour, the SEALs were engaged in an intense gun battle. In the battle, all but Luttrell were killed.

An MH-47 Chinook helicopter was dispatched with a force consisting of SEALs and 160th Special Operations Aviation Regiment Night Stalkers to rescue the team, but the helicopter was shot down. All 16 men on the Chinook were killed.

Badly wounded, Luttrell managed to walk and crawl 7 miles (11 km) to avoid capture. He was given shelter by a local Afghan tribe, who alerted the United States of his presence. U.S. forces finally rescued Luttrell six days after the gun battle.

Following his recovery from Operation Red Wings, Luttrell went back and completed one more mission before being retired. He then wrote a book, *Lone Survivor*. In 2014, his book was made into a hit movie starring the actor Mark Wahlberg.

Navy SEALs are trained to operate in difficult mountain terrain, such as that which Luttrell and his team experienced in Afghanistan.

SUPPORT TEAMS

For missions to be successful, SOF teams are made up of experts in many different fields, such as communications, weapons, engineering, and gathering and analyzing intelligence. Each expert has specialized training and is a valuable and crucial member of the team. They can advise on tactics, enemy positions, and how to deal with any number of threats to their lives and the lives of others. All members of the team have the same grueling training to become a SOF soldier before going on to train in specialist areas.

INTELLIGENCE AND COMMUNICATIONS

Knowledge can be a lifesaver when SOF units are on a mission. Intelligence experts gather and analyze crucial information and send it to the communications experts. The information is then passed on to the commanders who can assess situations and plan tactics. Communications soldiers are also responsible for the vital equipment that goes with the team on missions.

WEAPONS AND DEMOLITION

Weapons experts are trained in how to use not only their own weapons, but also those of their enemies. They also train fighters in other countries to use weapons. This is very important if they are building up a local army to help the other country's army in combat. On a mission, engineers can destroy military targets such as bridges and railroads, and they can build temporary bridges and other structures.

Marines must be comfortable using all kinds of weapons, not just those used by their own team.

This support medical team is treating a young Iraqi boy who has been burned.

MEDICAL BACKUP

SOF medics, such as doctors and nurses, are some of the best in the world. They can give lifesaving treatment to injured soldiers and civilians in combat zones. Injuries can be varied, so frontline medics also have training in dentistry and eye care. They also have some veterinary knowledge to help injured animals if necessary. In many countries, the water can cause severe sickness, and there may be deadly diseases among the local population. Medics are trained to provide information on any health issues that might be a danger to fighters.

SMALL BUT DANGEROUS

The United States Naval Special Warfare Command team operate around coastal areas and rivers. They support other SOFs, especially the SEALs, by conducting navigation, surveillance, and intelligence missions. Missions mainly involve taking SOF soldiers to and from dangerous missions. These soldiers use special watercraft that are small and quiet, so that they can be fast but also travel in secret. They are equipped with a wide range of deadly firearms and other specialized equipment.

Jonathan Johnson:

SOF MEDIC IN SYRIA

Jonathan Johnson is a U.S. SOF medic who served in Syria. He is not a fully trained doctor, but as a frontline medic, he was trained to deal with battlefield injuries of patients straight from the combat zones. During this service, Johnson treated many women and children who were innocent victims of the war raging around them.

Your FRONTLINE Career

Is Being a Medic for You?

Sounds Great

- Using your expert knowledge to make a difference to people's lives
- Working as part of a team that is caring, compassionate, and dedicated to helping others
- Solving health and hygiene problems that will have a positive long-term affect on local people

Things to Think About

- Seeing and dealing with horrendous injuries
- Working in almost impossible situations with limited medical equipment and medicine
- Giving medical assistance to the enemy as well as your own soldiers

Johnson's patients could be anyone from a soldier hit by an enemy sniper to a group of women and children blown up by a landmine. His mission was to treat their wounds and stop excessive bleeding. Patients were then taken by ambulance to the nearest hospital for further treatment and surgery, if necessary. One of the main aims of SOF medics is to treat all injured people the same way, with respect and kindness, whether they are the enemy, fellow soldiers, or civilians. As well as saving the lives of many injured as a result of the fighting, Johnson also did what he could to help the local community with noncombat health issues.

One day, a young girl named Sanaa arrived at the hospital gates with her family. Johnson was told that something was wrong with the girl, but he could not get any other information. Suddenly, a group of badly injured patients came in from the battlefield, so Johnson quickly went to tend to them. When there was a moment to spare, he hurried back to Sanaa and her family.

Sanaa was chatty and cheerful, but she had never walked. Her leg muscles were stiff, and she had no control over them. Johnson believed that she was suffering from a condition where muscles do not work properly because of brain damage.

Johnson could not treat her, and there was nowhere in Syria where the family could get that kind of help. However, his army training and quick thinking soon gave him an idea. He took a plastic stool and the wheels from a trash can outside. With the help of his colleagues, he attached the wheels to the stool with some tape to make a walker, so at least the girl could move around independently. This small action was life changing.

Johnson is proud of the fact that his SOF training and job with the army has given him the opportunity to use his skills to help develop respect and compassion between very different cultures and people.

On a training course, medics learn how to remove injured soldiers from dangerous combat zones before treating their injuries.

COULD YOU BE ON THE FRONTLINE?

Do you have what it takes to be a member of the SOF? Here are some of the key things to think about if you want a career in the special forces.

EDUCATION

To qualify for the U.S. and Canadian SOF, you first need to complete basic armed forces training and then additional specialized training. Qualifications to apply for basic training in the United States and Canada vary, depending on the branch of the armed forces.

TEAMWORK

You have to be able to work as part of a small team. Doing volunteer work in a team or being part of a sports team is good practice.

FITNESS

You need to be super fit to join the SOF. Do plenty of exercise, and eat a healthy diet. Try different types of exercises, such as running and weight training, to improve your strength and stamina. Being an excellent swimmer is also essential.

LEADERSHIP SKILLS

Commanding a team and working under pressure are necessary skills. Being captain of a sports team or taking on a leadership role at school will help develop these skills.

COMMITMENT

Training for the SOF is the toughest thing you will ever do. You need commitment to be able to keep going when you are mentally and physically exhausted. Say yes to challenges in your everyday life that will stretch you physically and mentally, especially fitness tests and those that involve teamwork.

VALUES

Think about how you treat your family and friends and how you behave. SOF operatives have to be honest, loyal, and brave. They have to have an interest in the world around them and be respectful of other cultures.

GLOSSARY

adapted Changed or adjusted to suit a new situation

ambush A surprise attack

armored vehicles Vehicles that are built with a tough exterior to help them survive enemy attacks

barricades Barriers put up to stop or delay the enemy

biological Describes germ warfare, which is a system of using deadly bacteria and viruses to attack people

chemical Describes warfare that uses chemical sprays, which can injure and kill people

classified Top secret information that is known by only a few people

communist Describes people or a country that believes in communism, a way of living that says everyone should share property and wealth

compound A group of buildings where people live and work, which is often surrounded by a high wall or fence

counterterrorism The fight against terrorism

culture The religion, art, and way of life of a people or country

elite The absolute best

guerilla A soldier or group who fights on their own, not under the command of an established army

hostage Someone who is held prisoner for money or political reasons

hostile Threatening and dangerous

humanitarian crises When a huge amount of suffering is caused to people, for example, when people become homeless and are without food and water because of a natural disaster

minesweeping Removing mines, which are explosive devices that have been dropped at sea

natural disasters Events caused by extreme weather, such as floods and hurricanes, in which people are left homeless and without food and water

navigation Finding one's way from one place to another, especially in unknown areas

negotiations Discussions aimed at reaching an agreement

nuclear Describes weapons that use deadly and destructive nuclear energy

peace workers People or organizations that work to bring peace to a place or to prevent violence

personnel The people who work for an organization or company

propaganda Information spread to promote a particular cause

radar A device that can pick up the position of a person or object using radio waves

radiological Related to deadly nuclear radiation

reconnaissance To secretly find out about enemy territory

resistance fighters People who fight for freedom against an enemy invading their country

Rules of Engagement (ROE) The rules that armies, navies, and air forces use in combat with opposing forces

sabotage To deliberately destroy or obstruct something

snipers People who shoot at targets from a long distance away

support personnel People who support others in many ways, such as by supplying them with information and first aid

tactics Plans or ways to achieve a specific goal

Taliban A violent religious group that wants to rule in Afghanistan

terrorists People or groups that use illegal fighting and violence, especially against people, to gain political or religious aims

undercover Secretly

urban Describes a town or city

warlord A military leader that controls a small area, usually within a country or state

LEARNING MORE

Discover more about the SOF and careers on the front line.

BOOKS

Doeden, Matt. *Can You Survive in the Special Forces?: An Interactive Survival Adventure* (You Choose: Survival). Capstone Press, 2012.

Labrecque, Ellen. *Special Forces* (Heroic Jobs). Capstone Global Library Ltd, 2013.

Levete, Sarah. *Special Forces* (Defend and Protect). Gareth Stevens, 2016.

Lusted, Amidon Marcia. *Army Delta Force: Elite Operations* (Military Special Ops). Lerner Publications, 2013.

Noll, Elizabeth. *Rank It: Special Ops Forces*. Black Rabbit Books, 2017.

Jeffrey, Gary Spender. *The Vietnam War* (Graphic Modern History: Cold War Conflicts). Crabtree Publishing, 2013.

WEBSITES

Learn more about the U.S. SOF, how to join them, and the training at:
www.goarmy.com/special-forces.html

Find out more about the Canadian SOF at:
www.canada.ca/en/special-operations-forces-command.html

For information about joining JTF 2, see:
www.canada.ca/en/special-operations-forces-command/corporate/ organizational-structure/joint-task-force-2.html

For a more detailed outline of the U.S. Army SOF training, go to:
www.military.com/special-operations/army-special-forces-training.html

INDEX

ABOUT THE AUTHOR

Sarah Eason has written books on many different subjects, from geography and history to science and art. In researching this book, she has learned about both the challenges and rewards of having a career on the frontline, and how those in service make a positive contribution to the lives of people all over the world.